MONTVILLE TWP. PUBLIC LIBRARY
90 HORSENECK ROAD
MONTVILLE, NJ 07045

050 2720

MORRIS AUTOMATED INFORMATION NETWORK

0 1021 0195552 8

W9-AQV-213

J 759.4
Flux
Flux, Paul.

Paul gauguin/

Montville Township Public Library
90 Horseneck Road
Montville, N.J. 07045-9626
973-402-0900
<u>**Library Hours**</u>

Monday	10 a.m.-9 p.m.
Tuesday	10 a.m.-9 p.m.
Wednesday	1 p.m.- 9 p.m.
Thursday	10 a.m.- 9 p.m.
Friday	10 a.m.- 5 p.m.
Saturday	10 a.m.- 5 p.m.
Sunday	1 p.m.- 5 p.m.

Closed Sundays July & August
see website   www.montvillelib.org

The Life and Work of...

Paul Gauguin

Paul Flux

Heinemann Library
Chicago, Illinois

© 2002 Reed Educational & Professional Publishing
Published by Heinemann Library,
an imprint of Reed Educational & Professional Publishing,
Chicago, Illinois
Customer Service 888-454-2279
Visit our website at www.heinemannlibrary.com

All rights reserved. No part of this publication may be reproduced or transmitted in any form or by any means, electronic or mechanical, including photocopying, recording, taping, or any information storage and retrieval system, without permission in writing from the publisher.

Designed by Celia Floyd
Illustrations by Peter Bull Art Studio
Originated by Ambassador Litho Ltd
Printed and bound in Hong Kong/China

06 05
10 9 8 7 6 5 4 3 2

Library of Congress Cataloging-in-Publication Data
Flux, Paul, 1952-
  Paul Gauguin / Paul Flux.
     p. cm. -- (The life and work of ...)
Summary: Presents a brief overview of the life and work of this French
artist, describing and giving examples of his work.
Includes bibliographical references and index.
  ISBN 1-58810-605-5 (lib. bdg.)   ISBN 1-4034-0004-0 (pbk. bdg.)
 1. Gauguin, Paul, 1848-1903--Juvenile literature. 2.
Painters--France--Biography--Juvenile literature. [1. Gauguin, Paul,
1848-1903. 2. Artists. 3. Painting, French.] I. Title. II. Series.
  ND553.G27 F62 2002
  759.4--dc21

                              2001003968

Acknowledgments
The author and publishers are grateful to the following for permission to reproduce copyright material:
p. 4, Roger Viollet, Paris; p. 7, AKG; p. 9, N.Y. Carlsberg Glyptotek, Copenhagen; pp. 11, 19, 29, Musée d'Orsay, Paris; p. 13, Bridgeman Art Library; p. 15, Goteborgs Konstmuseum; p. 16, Mary Evans Picture Library; p. 17, National Gallery of Scotland, Edinburgh; pp. 20, 23, Amsterdam, Van Gogh Museum (Vincent van Gogh Foundation); p. 21, Stedelijk Museum, Amsterdam; pp. 24, 26, Roger Viollet Collection; p. 25, N.Y. Carlsberg Glyptotek, Copenhagen; p. 27, Metropolitan Museum of Art, New York; p. 28, Corbis.

Cover photograph (*Tahitian Women [On The Beach]*, Paul Gauguin) reproduced with permission of Giraudon/Musée d'Orsay.

Every effort has been made to contact copyright holders of any material reproduced in this book. Any omissions will be rectified in subsequent printings if notice is given to the publisher.

Special thanks to Katie Miller for her comments in the preparation of this book.

Some words are shown in bold, **like this.** You can find out what they mean by looking in the glossary.

0 1021 0195552 8

09/15/05
HtL
$ 17.75

Contents

Who Was Paul Gauguin?

Paul Gauguin was one of the most important painters of his time. He lived and painted in places far away. Most people who bought his art had never seen these places.

4

Paul did not paint things to look real. Everything in his pictures looks flat. He painted with the bright colors he saw in **tropical** flowers.

Tahitian Landscape, 1893

5

Early Years

Paul was born in Paris, France, on June 7, 1848. In 1849 Paul and his family went to live with his mother's family in Lima, **Peru.** His father died during the trip.

The Artist's Mother, 1889

Paul, his sister Marie, and their mother lived in Lima until Paul was seven. In 1855 they went back to France. Paul painted this picture of his mother many years after she died.

Sailing and a Family

When he was only seventeen years old, Paul became a sailor. He sailed the world for six years, seeing many faraway places. He went back to Paris in 1871.

In 1873 Paul married Mette Gad. They had four sons named Emile, Clovis, Jean, and Pola, and a daughter named Aline. This picture shows Paul's young family.

The Artist's Family in the Garden, Rue Carcel, 1881–82

The Modern Artist

In 1874, Paul met the artist Camille Pissarro. He became Paul's friend and teacher. Paul began to take painting more seriously. He later was part of a special **exhibition** in Paris.

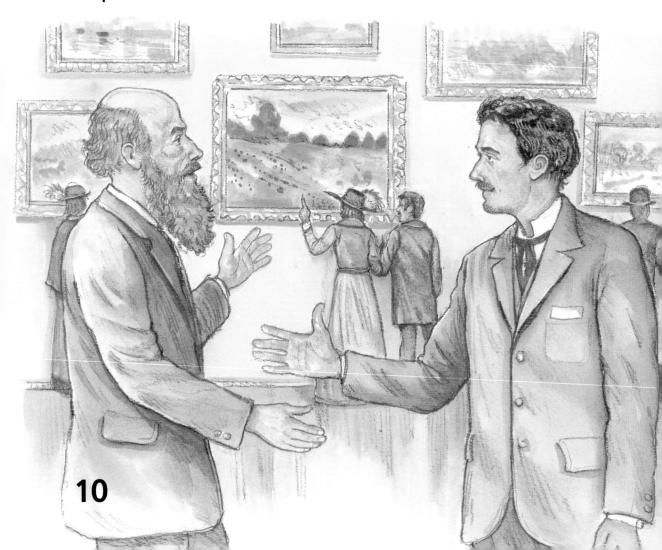

The Seine at the Pont d'Iéna, Snowy Weather, 1875

Paul and Camille both had **Impressionist** styles in the beginning. Both went on to develop their own painting styles. Paul began painting **landscapes,** like this one.

Working in Paris

Paul worked in an office in Paris. He was good at his job and made enough money to care for his family. He did not enjoy his work, though.

The Garden in Winter, Rue Carcel, 1883

Paul painted in his spare time. He became less and less interested in his job. He was asked to show his paintings at another **exhibition**. He sent this picture of his family in their garden.

Other Artists

In 1883 Paul lost his job. He decided to try painting **full time.** He wanted to be part of the group of artists working in Paris, like Claude Monet and Paul Cézanne.

In 1884 Paul moved his family to **Copenhagen,** Denmark. The next year he left them there and returned to Paris. In the summer of 1886, Paul painted this view of Brittany in France.

Seascape, 1886

On the Panama Canal

Paul had wanted to live in **tropical** countries for some time. In 1887 he left France with a friend. Together they worked on the building of the **Panama Canal**.

After working on the canal, Paul visited the island of **Martinique** for the first time. He liked the bright light and colors he found there. He painted this picture of what he saw.

Martinique Landscape, 1887

17

Back in France

When Paul returned to France in 1887 he was very ill. He had little money. He lived with a friend, Emile Schuffenecker, and his family.

The Schuffenecker Family, 1889

Later, Paul stayed with them again and painted this picture of the family. Emile is shown in the background. He looks like he is not really part of the family.

Vincent van Gogh

Paul left Paris again in 1888. He went to live in this house in Arles, France. He lived with Vincent van Gogh, another painter. They agreed to paint **portraits** of each other.

20

Paul painted Vincent working on one of his most famous pictures. Vincent was very unhappy at this time in his life. He only lived for two more years.

Van Gogh Painting Sunflowers, 1888

A Terrible Argument

On the day Paul finished his **portrait** of Vincent, the two men had an argument. Vincent threw a glass into Paul's face. Paul decided to leave Arles.

Les Miserables, 1888

This self-portrait was Paul's favorite. He liked the strange colors in it. Paul gave this painting to Vincent before they argued.

23

Off to Tahiti

In 1891 Paul visited his family in **Copenhagen**
for the last time. He was unhappy and decided
to leave France. He went to live on the island
of **Tahiti,** in the Pacific Ocean.

24

This is one of the first **portraits** Paul did of a person from Tahiti. She is wearing her very best clothes. Paul felt he could paint with greater freedom in Tahiti than in Europe.

Woman with a Flower, 1891

A Time of Sadness

In 1893 Paul returned to Paris. He held a show of his paintings to make some money. He used the money to rent a new **studio** instead of sharing the money with his family.

Paul returned to **Tahiti** again. In April 1897, he found out that his daughter had died of **pneumonia** earlier in the year. She was only twenty. Paul never really got over her death.

Mother and Daughter, 1901–1902

Last Days

Paul died on May 8, 1903, after being ill for a long time. He had not reached the level of success he felt he deserved. After Paul's death, more people began to appreciate his work.

Paul's pictures of the people of Tahiti are among the best that he ever painted. Paul developed his **Post-Impressionist** style over time and created many great works of art.

The Meal (The Bananas), 1891

Timeline

1848	Paul Gauguin is born on June 7 in Paris, France.
1849	Paul's family leave France to live in **Peru**. His father dies on the journey.
1865	Paul becomes a sailor and goes to sea on the ship *Luzitano*.
1871	He begins work in an office in Paris.
1872	Paul starts to paint on Sundays as a hobby.
1873	He marries a Danish woman named Mette Gad.
1874	He meets Camille Pissarro. Paul's first child is born; a boy named Emile.
1876	Paul has a painting shown at a special **exhibition** in Paris.
1883	Paul suddenly loses his job. He begins to paint **full time**.
1885	Paul leaves his family.
1887	He leaves France and works on the **Panama Canal**. He visits **Martinique** and paints twelve pictures.
1888	Paul stays with Vincent van Gogh in Arles for two months, but leaves after an argument.
1890	Vincent van Gogh dies.
1891	Paul arrives in **Tahiti** for the first time.
1893	He leaves Tahiti to return to France. He lives and works in Paris.
1895	Paul leaves France for Tahiti again. He never returns to France.
1897	Paul's daughter, Aline, dies. Paul is very unhappy.
1903	He dies on May 8 at the age of 54.

Glossary

Copenhagen   capital city of Denmark

exhibition   public display of works of art

full time   to do something as a job every workday

Impressionists   group of artists who showed the effect of light and movement in their pictures

landscape   picture of the countryside

Martinique   island of the West Indies, in the Atlantic Ocean

ordered   told to do something by an official

Panama Canal   canal that links the Atlantic and Pacific oceans

Peru   large country in South America

pneumonia   disease that affects the lungs

portrait   painting of a person

Post-Impressionist   style of painting that built on the Impressionist style of painting

studio   room or building where an artist works

Tahiti   large island in the Pacific Ocean

tropical   describes a hot, wet place where many plants grow easily

Index

More Books to Read

Connolly, Sean. *The Life and Work of Vincent van Gogh.* Chicago: Heinemann Library, 2000.

Goldman Rubin, Susan and Joseph A. Smith. *The Yellow House.* Chicago: Abrams, 2001.

Spence, David. *Gauguin.* Hauppauge, N.Y.: Barron's, 1994.

More Artwork to See

*A Farm in Brittany.*1894. Metropolitan Museum of Art, New York, N.Y.

Breton Girls Dancing, Pont-Aven. 1888. National Gallery of Art, Washington, D.C.

Madame Alexander Kohler. 1887–88. National Gallery of Art, Washington, D.C.

MONTVILLE TWP. PUBLIC LIBRARY
90 HORSENECK ROAD
MONTVILLE, NJ 07045